The Thinking Heart

By the same author

poetry

The Unlooked-for Season
Rose in the Afternoon

for children

Boots
Wheels
Water
Wind
Tea
Sunday

The Thinking Heart

Jenny Joseph

Secker & Warburg · London

First published in England 1978 by
Martin Secker & Warburg Limited
54 Poland Street, London W1V 3DF

436 22800 9

To my children,
preventers of literature, life-savers

Printed in Great Britain by
REDWOOD BURN LIMITED
Trowbridge & Esher

Contents

For a new year   7
Two elements   8
Tides   9
Married people going to work   10
Anthropomorphism reversed   11

Altarpiece   12

Animal stories   19
Love and Justice   21
Trying to understand violence   22
Lost hold   23
Meeting up   24

The Goddess of Nature's diatribe to her people   26

Against the personality cult   29
The allotted time   30
Scene   32
Points failure. A conversation   33

Life and Turgid Times of A. Citizen   36

Lure   56
An instant on the viaduct   56
Tug   57
On the Nature of Scientific Law   58
Figure in a landscape   58
Upside down   59

Acknowledgments

Some of these poems have previously been published by *Ambit, Bananas,* the BBC, *Cracked Looking Glass, Encounter, Green Lines, The Listener, The New Statesman, PN Review, Poetry Review, The Scotsman, TR, Vole,* and the Mandeville Press.

Jenny Joseph acknowledges the generous assistance of the Arts Council of Great Britain.

For a new year

Time heals, you said.
It moves, I amended.

But really time fills in:
The great sore ditch running across the field
Bunged full of rubble, of any that comes to hand,
A lumpy scar, dead section down through the land,
In time gets trampled flat, in time glows over
With fresh light grass, and all sorts of little flowers.

Sometimes you see a meadow with a strange bright pathway:
The skin of a weal is delicate and thin.

Here is a place they have been laying pipes
Making, behind the hedge, a muddy desert
That the wind will bleach and set into dry crests.
What are all those little white flowers doing
Twinkling in the clods the men have thrown
Any old how? Have they roots at all?
Or is it the sun flashing on shards of china?

From here they could be flowers or bits of china
Or scraps of litter from some paper chase.
Head to one side and squint, they look like flowers.
Are they the fields', native? will they
Come up again next year when the land has settled?
Or strangely flourish this once, and leave no growth?
Let the wind work for us
Oh let it blow
All the loose dust away, and let
What then can —
Grow.

Two elements

There I was, awash on the river of love
Laved and left rolling
And the tide went out.
Was there not somewhere, I said, like sea
Where boat and water are always there together?
There is the sea, they said, are you ocean going?
I don't see as you'd make it in that wreck
And you've missed the season.

Is there no element then, I said, like lakes
Constant to keep a barque up?
Dependable so one may use one's compass
Charts, rigging, for what they were bought for?

Wait, some said, the river will come back.
We know this river, they said, it has always
Gone out and come in, and we adapt ourselves.
All I know is it was damned uncomfortable
Adapting
Keeling over like that, perched high above
The only thing available when the tide goes out —
Green mud and rusty cans.

Others advised "get off if you have the chance.
Make it to the sea and I swear you'll never regret it.
That's what I'd do if I were you, only
I know this river and it seems to suit me.
Of course I'd come and help you out and . . . only . . ."

They knew the river
All I know is that
A boat needs water.

A sailor comes and "with the next high tide
I'll come aboard.
The estuary's tricky and you'll get no joy

From the river people. They want you to stay here
So they don't feel there's better out beyond."
He turned up at the Springs. We lifted off
With a bump or two, and past the misty banks
Slipped like the middle years, poignant, unmarked
Our moving of no consequence
To either bank.
There lay the great expanse of the only sea.
From having been part of the coastline, part of the scene
That fringed the shore where things could start, go back,
Ambiguous, amphibious, gradually we stood off
And found ourselves in only that limitless stretch
That boundaries everything.
No further stages to linger or embark at
Nowhere to go to and no going back
For we were in it now.
The timbers slapped against the endless hours
That came with the waves — on and on and on.
The plate of the horizon could not change
For we moved in it, it contained us so
In a perpetual now, as sharp, and cold
As each separate drop of water that slid back
Off of our rigging into the inseparable sea.

Tides

There are some coasts
Where the sea comes in spectacularly
Throwing itself up gullies, challenging cliffs,
Filling the harbours with great swirls and flourish,
A theatrical event that people gather for
Curtain up twice daily. You need to know
The hour of its starting, you have to be on guard.

There are other places
Places where you do not really notice
The gradual stretch of the fertile silk of water
No gurgling or dashings here, no froth no pounding
Only at some point the echo may sound different
And looking by chance one sees "Oh the tide is in."

Married people going to work

When I am going on journeys
Drawing through the suburbs in a train
Like one clear thread in a garment of heather tweed,
We seem to be cutting into new territory; new faces
Lap against one's vision, people doing
Different things from us, or at different times.

I have left you, and the little stones I see
Beside the track are not shining in your day.
Of the roadside faces and the clothes the people wear
A window flashing, men stopped for an accident,
The encounters and sights that feed you on your way
I cannot be, for hours, participant.

But the world is round.
The track of love I travel brings me back
To a station where we have been
Where you stand and wait, holding out your hand
All the goods of your day on offer
In exchange for all that I have seen.

Anthropomorphism reversed

The vacant lot has long been vacant.
When the mask of frost that here furs over
Disgusting things, anaesthetizing rot,
Shall have seeped away in pools, leaving
Perhaps a green of grass in other places
This tumble of bricks, bottle bottoms, cracked tarpaulins, dog
bones
Black bones of scaffolding propping one side of this strange
garden
Will be as indistinct, as unlustrous
Wearied beyond even stench, one feels, — decomposition too
active for it —
As now when iron cold pre-empts colour and movement.
Then even moist limp yellow straggles
Of old Summer's grass lying on stones like hair
Will have lost any gleam or grip.

But I look at it after
Days in the grey womb of a fog-like house,
Protected, beating slowly only, in sleep.
I look at the utterly frozen countryside
That strangely has these sheds and buildings on it
Not seeming like a town, no movement shows
Except the distant slicing blades of light
That fall, glass icicles, from the wide open sky.

And I think, if a pushing season can change our hearts
And birds and buds effect a loosening
Before the earth is ready to thaw or stir
Could human hearts in love bring on the season
As all our breaths in separate rooms in London
Must warm a segment of the atmosphere
Making a pocket of another climate
Where hyacinth can bloom and limbs uncurl?

ALTARPIECE

Study: A lady in her bedroom (Bonnard)

"Mirror mirror on the wall
Who is the most beautiful?"
If you hear the answer "You are",
It doesn't come from the mouth in the mirror

That shapes not words but silent kisses
To someone not there.

From hands the answer rises,
As you rise from the bed
Making no noise, no interruption
They move over you in the air
As wax coats cheese,
They stand you up shining there
Before the mirror
Shaping and preserving you as beautiful
Because they feel you so
That you see through what the eye says
To the body the hands have made
And this it is that prays
"I am, I am."

Interior: The man turns the sheet for the musician (Dutch)

Too many beautiful women lie alone in bed.
The mirror gives no answer to these, the air
In boxes where one human breathes, grows withered
And cannot carry an echo through the room
In answer to the question "Am I fair?"
Fair . . .

Only the use of beauty will preserve
Your beauty.
The vampire lust sucks bodies limp and lightless
But my desire will silver the mirror where
Your new-lit eyes, not seeing, will declare:
(From any unadorned, uncastled wall)
"Made in my image, while you look at me
The answer to your open mouth must be:
'You are the fairest of them all.' "

Landscape: Jungle Days (Dutch)

It is good to attend to the flesh and groom the pelt —
So smile the smile of the cat that has licked the cream —
And grin with the tiger that has swallowed the hunter —
And laugh and glow with these young men at the ready
All smoothed for Saturday night.

For it is complicity with death the enemy
To undermine those reinforcements
Drummed up to reassure the population;
To be a rat that gnaws through the sandbags
Stacked, generation after generation, to harden
Into a wall against the desert's onslaught.
O do not say this is not the defence that's needed
Nor point out the futility of setting sand to sand:
It has been used for years and is acceptable.

Be happy therefore with the lingering postman, pleased to
                                          present
The envelope (pools win?) to housewife in doorway.
She leans with her house open — warm street, warm welcome.
Summer is here, shut no doors now, we say;
Pass on the happy cliché and it might turn true.

Never mind who gets the whey
We don't know the hunter
It wouldn't be one of *our* wives young men go after
(For see, we will join them and of our share make certain).

We have kept out the desert for *our* green to flourish
We have trained and suffered —
Not to learn how we can live off rock
If that should prove to be all there is left to live off,
But to grab a valley where and when we can.

So if you have chanced to see a cat with a bird
That flaps its wings with its head stuck down the cat's throat,
If you have seen a mauled and gangrened arm
And smelt its ripped cargo rotting in the lianas

Think of the worm
Think of the bloodstained beasts.
It is their nature to do so, is it not in yours?

And if your talent is to smell the rot
To know where the cat has been, lithe creature, and divine
What happens in lodging houses in the week —
What the young men look like when they cram their mouths,
Don't tell the children the things mirages come from.
They may need one to get them across the desert,
And miss the sweet mouthful that could have kept them
                                                  going.

But wise and ugly, circumvent the ice
On which the eleven day feastings have been set.
It is good to attend to the flesh but the Thames melted.
Solid as that the mirror in whose blue veins
Shine the smile of the cat, the grin of the tiger
The nice fat woman at her door, promising,
And the glow that their movement strikes from the limbs of
                                                  the workers.

Allegory: Old man's fancy (Poussin)

If I could slide my hand over your thighs
Fashioning round the haunches of the land,
Smooth green pelt that rises to my touch
From the white headland chalk bones that I finger,
The young trees opening to my loving breath —

But only rain and sun can make the grass grow
And I am an old man now.

If I could lie on the beds of your running rivers
Stretching my limbs through the valley folds to your farms
Secret in woods far from the wind off the sea —
(The giants in those days had bones that, turned to chalk,
Became these hills)
And let your waters pour down over me
Winter and Summer till I calcified
Like a statue on the stones,
Perhaps the juice that fattens out the grasses
Would strengthen me and liquefy my veins
And I would breed a race of beauties
Living by your streams among your woods
Offspring of god and land,
Standing on your bare hills with their long hair gleaming
Blowing about them in the blustery winds,
My bones beneath their feet.

But only life can make the living grow
And I am an old man now.

Sitting in the car with the window down
At the spot my children brought me, to see the view,
I cannot even bend to feel the earth
Covered in its green fur, dry and springy.

My giant appetites towards this land
Are greater than its children need to feel
For they are of it and I love them too —
Soft creatures I have brought out of the grass,
My nymphs, my grandsons who content each other
And do not know the racking of the Sky God
Pressing on his more than human earth.

Centrepiece: St Sebastian (Italian)

Faith struck Sebastian, got him
Hands twisted behind his back,
His heart thrust out
And other vulnerable parts he could not cover.

Now see Sebastian a prisoner there
The archer's patron by the archers hit
The soft white skin no day had looked upon
All parts exposed before the clothed crowd
Stretched for the tough little darts and the shafts of eyes
Armpits and groin tied open for their arrows.

The arrow of lust has hit him where it hurts
And he has no protection, for he looks
Upward into another element.
Died for the cause, for preaching love to men
Caught by the unconverted, no defence
And all his caring turned against him now.
Love tied his hands. He cannot catch the darts
Hurtling towards him and return them back.

It is not hand alone that shoots the shaft
Into the entrails of the body of love.
It was the word of Brutus, not the sword
Left Caesar undefended.
The word, like the barb on the shaft, feathers the dart
And fixes it in the skin against withdrawal.

They left him dead, relieved to have rooted out
The alien soldier from their body of men.

But love that stood him there thought otherwise.
Strange the seeping word, for lo at night
Sebastian carried to a little place
Where quiet and sure his wounds he struggles from
Helped by good women, fleshly life long done.
Set forth again by kindness on his voyage
Straightway to General Diocletian went
"Your servant, left for dead, reporting, Sir,
Ready for service, for see how little harmed
By arrows of the world my intent was.
You must believe me now, for here I stand."
"His head it is supplies his lusty flesh
With all this lofty life and resurging.
Batter it then and see if *that* survives;
And pulp his secret on the cobblestones."

Portrayed again and this time on a boat
Hands tied behind his back, glazed figurehead
Breasting the wave with white flesh, cherry lips
And freshly glossy dark black cherry ringlets.
Figurehead for heroic acts, bright log
That faltering worshippers tie their goodness to.
So let the ship depart on its endless voyage
Cracked and warped as it is with the summer pestilence
That swells tongues in the back streets of the town
That bloats the corpses in the sewers thrown,
Ricocheting disease, flesh stuck to flesh
Clinging to what it takes its fever from.

So out to its plate of water where no land
Can ever creep up round the horizon, where salt
Dries out the festers, shrinks flesh, where the thongs crack
And Sebastian's hands burst free. Above his head
They soar, and like a swallow flashing
His body shoots from the deck. In a perfect dive

His encrusted body of death he draws through the green
Green wave. The mighty ocean takes him.
At last upon his proper element
Embarked, immersed in waters, laved in love
He can make use of all adversity.
Buoyed up with salt and love, O he rides over
Six little waves to roll in each seventh seventh.

"O all you worshippers, locked far inland
O you may keep the images of my flesh
And let help who it may; the rigours of love
I have gone through have freed me to a life
To use my body as I know it best,
Not bodiless adoration, but embodied
In every turn and twist, the dolphin's lair,
Directed by the thinking heart, so now
I run with the tide, and this great tide runs high,
This is true worship, to breathe, to act, to be
Part of this running tide, in love set free."

The much-garbed painted crowd cling to each other
Pointing and looking at the empty hill for their saint.
Far off between the hills at the end of the picture
The noonday sun sparkles on the little waves.

Animal Stories

No wuffling
No scuffling
No scraping
No scuttering
Could ever have come from this still morsel
Brown like a clod of earth, but with the sudden appearance
Of an animal. I almost stepped on it.
A live mouse will suddenly be there, you do not see him
                                                    coming
But where did this rigid thing that could never have moved
Arrive from, what joker set it down among my stones?
It is too perfect in its awful stillness,
Each hair remarkable, more perfect than any toy
But with the exactness of something never alive.
No breath could have moved the skin about over this body.

The iron frost held for three days.
We kept close, not opening the back door:
Time enough when pipes unfreeze to see to things.
But we cannot imagine a Will ever pulsing again.
Lie low, wait, emptied of action
Emptied by the iron in the sky
That is blanching life out into its pole of darkness.

I suppose it broke eventually, the cold:
But nobody came, no one disturbed the yard
No bird, no cat, no change of light in the desert
Of frozen hard-stuck rubble.
All I remember is at last going out
To see about the mouse.

The body was gone that so inert had been.
No little bit, no outline, left behind.
Absence only.

Do our dead selves come and go like this through the black
Cold night of our desertion,
Harbouring what hidden diseases who can tell,
Dislocated from the killed feelings that made them live?

Love and Justice
(To Barbara Grant-Adamson)

Justice we ask
From grey-clad, clean-lined figures,
Not talking overmuch, standing in line
Or sitting upright, looking with a clear stern gaze;
The known; and we can take it — no tooth and claw —
To give us what we say we want: our rights,
To see to it that each gets his deserts.
You can count quite clearly what there is to pay.
We nod, draw in our breaths, and do without thereafter.

Justice is all we *can* ask:
To feel we can reckon the number of stairs, the length of the
                                                      passage
That the world is knowable and can be tamed
That we compete for a place in that strange bed
Where every traveller's fitted, and cripples made.

With justice we can claim.
Without it there's no road that isn't mined,
But darks and deeps and stumbling off the track —
We don't expect to be supported *there.*

But when the moon sails clear of encroaching cloud
And seems to show a firm dry road ahead
Oh who would not rather run to love than justice?
Procrustes' guests and Cinderella's sisters
Could after all not walk in the streets or dance.
Justice keeps up a world based not on love.
Without its hardcore we should sink in the bog.
You cannot ask for what is sometimes given
Nor claim, but hope, for more than you deserve
When you visit the hunched inexact domain of love.

Trying to understand violence

The fly is not a nuisance to itself
It is fat and beautiful to its own kind.
Happily it hovers over the meat
Taking off with bounces, buzzing with joy.

In the heat the pavements blotched and stained
Stink with the market offal, and the flies
Cluster round the garbage and our legs.
They will choke us if we do not kill them.
Ugh! they are crowding over the food, inserting eggs
Into the meat and smearing it with danger.

To hurt humans is quite different, they do not
Rot our substance; the bayonetted babies
And other innocents thrown to the cobblestones
Did not threaten the soldiers; but those men
Had been told they did; taught disgust
They swatted them like flies; the eggs would grow
Into a horde to over-run their land.

This sticky gritty wind infects the air
The streets are full of vermin, and ugh! — these flies.

Lost hold

I stepped from a bank with sea pink and long tufts
Of separate grasses, the blue day all about me.
Between two steps I saw the earth so clear
Each grain separately winking, heard every leg
Of insect creaking, and every worm that breathed.
And in the cradle of my mind I held —
As I might nestle a perfect stone in my palm —
The open secret of the world at large.

And edged as was the bright sky was my mind
With clear and solving ever-meaning words
The kernel of this great truth greatly to show.

Two steps along the track and the words had gone
The day and grasses faded to a beauteous
Example only of a lovely land.
My pebble out of water has no lustre;
Seems, shown to you, to have no point at all.
The shore is dark now, my mind gone again
But somewhere must the pulse of light be lurking
Pushing at flaws to break through. Is it under the skin
Of the stone, or wrapped in the mesh of the mind?
Is there a good sharp blade to cut it free?

Meeting up

See, it is all one thing, now, this meadow.
The cows strolling about have lain down in focus
It is perfectly right there are more here than there.
The bird is flying into, not over, the centre.
Canals thick-standing in static air, meander
With just direction and pull the grasses together,
The hummocks, the flitting butterflies, the cowpats.
From the right hand of this picture comes a tractor.
Its sound lassoos these objects as the track
It's going along frames the field, and winds
Through the wood off left. You cannot see
But know it goes out again, and comes back round
As arms of love hold in eccentric movements.

And look, we're here now, me, myself and I
And parts and pieces unanimously stand.
Bits pared off on the way, components dispersed
Attributes, intentions, seemlinesses,
Stripped off, stamped underfoot (and the skin grows over)
Caught up mysteriously across the years,
Creeping where no path showed, where I thought
Unmaintained and functionless they'd rotted
Into the waste-tip of the severed past.

I stare at the water-meadows to grasp, to hoard
The whole within the glass before it blurs
And from this centre send my mind's rope in
Increasing circles to include this boat
This mud-flat, now the island, even the slope
Beyond the estuary on the other side —
Not added but included.
The cows, cowpats, hummocks, grasses, birds
Are as they were.
They are no more unified
Than every separate beanflower in the field
That in their difference pulled my mind apart
In earlier years.
                    They
Are as they are. The stanchions of my thought
Have drawn them in together to reflect
The monolith I need to circle round,
To hold the deep-sea netting of my mind.

The Goddess of Nature's diatribe to her people

So you thought those gorgeous lips were for you to use?
Made for tasting, made to bring you delight
And equally to those who gaze and kiss?

You think that rose
Unfurling petals stiff with creamy life
Is for the onlookers to rest their eyes on!
That the clambering lily shaking off the mud,
Fun in back streets,
Love out of suffering
Is the apogée of mud, slums, suffering.

Why should I wonder that you are such fools
Since even this foolishness I planted in you?
Your pleasures are planted on you like Nessus' shirt.
Screaming with agony you tear at threads
That nowhere are removable. To move
Back up the worn moist step that you slipped from
Into the liquors of the hypnotic flower,
Would pull your flesh off; body, the self's clothing
Meshes your substance at your every wriggle.

Look at those insects drowning at the heart of my flowers.

Think to avoid me? Going to get the honey
Without the sulphurous smoke and swollen hands?
Think to refine the juice of love from its smell
By breeding out the strains that bind you so?
Whichever came first the egg is not a by-product
Of hen who lives a separate life as hen.

Nothing's for fun — for my convenience only.
Little ants, toiling up a self-made hill
What gratifies that you meet, oh savour it
But do not turn and bask in it as aim.

Pursuit of pleasure leaves you trapped in duty
My slaves.
One little brush against the sticky side
And down you go into the seething centre.

An answer from her goblin

I work in your kitchens
Yes, I am your creature
I see as much of the sky as you want me to
You raise your eyebrow and my left toe twitches
I run up and down clattering at your commanding.

But listen here, old bitch, tho' I know you've got me
I forget, on occasions, I'm bred in your arrangements
And I have valued the bent and awkward and have not
                                                    ministered
Always to the strong.
I have not at every point slavered
At the lips for pleasure in front of beautiful witches.

Tyrant, in your accounting you have forgotten kindness
The little decencies between spent beings
Tending each ordinary heart
Wrapping the sobbing body in the soft blanket
Of everyday thoughts from those who grieve alongside.
"I too" the broken say "I understand.
Come and rest and gain a little courage."
I stoke the fires. I follow the regime.
But I am storing up my fighting fund.

The Goddess goes on regardless

Extraordinary defences against Me!
I'll get you born, I'll make you stretch to the light
I'll let that light corrode you.
All that lovely food you champed and champed
Not able to resist, the tongue salivering,
Dripping to merge with the juices of delight,
Spurting from greed to greed not satisfaction,
Has gnawed you as it fed you, and at the root
Of your devouring appetite the weevil of pain
Is sitting waiting in bone's antechamber
To burrow into the instruments that demanded
More and more pleasure — organs, glands and fibres.
My torture chambers wait for those who turn
And equally for those who fawn on me.
Nothing but hazard can keep you from my rake
And even that mindless wheel is spun by me.
My logic is that fact should follow fact
Only "it is so" sounds through all my kingdom.

A grinding work for nothing but waste, you say?
And where have you seen peaches and dawns like mine?

Against the personality cult

Kind of you, sunshine, to come out just now
As if for us, materials for pattern making
Suddenly laid to hand.

The thought is that someone in control
Is sensitive and amiable to our needs.
The point of patterns is to be thorough, to recur, to
                                        conclude.
This one goes on: sun mist dark dull days, and open eyes
When we are nowhere.

So shine, sun, bless you, but not for us.
Shine only, and I hope I'll be there.

The allotted time

The allotted time for the return of ghosts
Is it plotted
Along a graph of time; as on a map
The place to meet is here where two roads cross
Or there by the station incline?

The blood spattered on the lorry head
The mud
Tossed up when the cab ploughed its windscreen through the
ditch
Marks for succeeding years the accident
The lorry moves under.

Is there some substance behind bright circles
In the air
Staring eyes that look in the light can make —
Thickening breath, or shapes against the sky
To warn us in time?

You cannot by longing make a ghost appear,
Nor by forethought
Force him not to. I can or needn't go
To the roadside meeting, but how can we avoid
Junctions in time?

We move on a road jammed by moments
That follow us.
Others pursue and hound us along our route.
When from the swirling black of the fields at the side,
Stood in the headlights,

Appear — pleading, luring, dementing,
Too near —
The gestures of a figure, oh covey of ghosts
How can I give your representative due welcome?
You've no real kingdom.

If I make obeisance to you and lead off the road
Over the bank
I shall wake only in the charred sticks of the dead,
Not the faint palaces that sometimes seem
Clearer than earth I tread.

Scene

O far across the pebbles there you stand.
The moves you make seem somehow not towards me —
Floundering up to my ankles in sliding stones.

The mist that creeps over my feet wraps round
A figure by what might have been a jetty.
It spreads and closes, leaving hardly six inches
For black cobbles, shiny with wet, to be clear on the ground.
The ash-grey shores of fog roll round my head
Someone beyond it moves the other way.

I come to my senses in sweet air. You are gone —
You or whoever it was that seemed to be there.

This was no dream, dear,
Nor no fever spot,
Nor image sent to save
When you would not:
There are pictures
That are always there
But they blot out
In our own air.

If I should see you, talking, turning, smiling
In clothes that have colour, as most fabrics do,
And ruddy skin, bright eyes that throw back light
I shall be only on that desert causeway
Four or five dark cobbles at my feet —
Nothing else visible, quite devoid of sound —
A wet path wandering in an emptied town
Unlit by docks, ending at black water.

Points failure. A conversation

In all the dark and dirty ways I go
Iron passages with puddles on the floor
Old soot scored through to the metal with fresh abuse
The only recent thing here the weekend's litter
Very soon soiled, and a few bright signs
At ticket offices, unmanned, unhaunted.
Nicely-clothed people holding the morning's paper
Hair done, skin cleaned, clad from shops where they lavish
The latest maintenance on the display dummies
Thread through these plated bridges to their every day.
A couple of old men, picks across backs,
Tend what's left of the railway, down at the level
In an unused siding, a disconnected world.

All these passengers
Sit and wait while frost has sealed the points
Sleek crows gutting a system. And then trussed chickens.
No one opens a window. No one moves.
Money and effort's gone beyond the hill
Shearing into the pasture the railway left,
Slabbing huge concrete structures that stand, rust-dribbled,
Blocks there's not money for to make beautiful
Or even finish. Hospital wings stand empty
Away from the town denied its blood to build them.
What's left of the nurses that could have manned them, now
Model for adverts of medical text books and gear.
The special features of the landscape here
Are piles of cars that no one finds worth mending.
Some have only a screw loose — five miles away
Old people and kids hump washing through the streets
And boxes the sleek middle-aged refuse as too heavy.

But climbing behind this rubbish — what a morning!
What burnished light from trees along the track
Whose leaves cling in the still air, vestigially,
To the jointures of twigs withdrawing the last connection.
What delicacy, what glory these reds, these browns!

So something will renew, you say, and decay
(Brown mulch) will shelter the roots and keep alive
What will be green and sprouting another season?
But will this do? You can't make soil from cans
Or consume through a light-giving flame these plastic bags
Dripping and slimed with dog muck.
We've made a world but can't construct its physics.
We've built an atmosphere we can control
No more than the clouds, the rain that falls, the drought,
The drop in temperature, the shift in rock.

    Sun will rise, or not,
    And sleet will fall;
    Grass sprout
    Through the wall
    Why should you think
    One cog in the wheel can hold
    The structures it helps turn,
    In command?
    Look at our climate now
    Yes, we have made this weather
    But grass does not pull the sun
    Cog does not rule the wheel
    Users and dog shit cannot make more land.

    You mind that they don't mind, these scavengers?
    And why complain? The medieval farmer
    Huddled in cold and dark and poverty.
    And was crowded into the filth with pigs, like us,
    And had small speech.
    He fought his enemies, the natural plagues,
    And made false gods to help him in his struggle.

The sun that lit the birches is rising now
And since it lies in its path, has warmed the metal.
The dummies in the train think it is mended.
Some vow to use their cars, others rehearse
Ritual excuse for being late at the office.
Has no one heard
The crumbling of the idols in the sand?
Do they *want* to be crushed in the crowd by the huge
                                                    stanchions
Flaking beneath roads leading to nowhere fast?

The train's movement stirs us, jolts the vision.
People get out of the carriages into the streets
And things get done, and the journey joins the dreams.
But just before my station sheathed the train
And I leapt out to the busy day ahead
A rusty flange made an outline in a puddle
Of oil spreading in a breaker's yard:
A woman in a garb, and a small child
Dragging a cooking pot across a plain.

LIFE AND TURGID TIMES OF A. CITIZEN

Proem: Against metaphor — but how then?

I am not going to talk to you about islands
Or about waving grasses.
I am not going to mention the lakes that the moon fills
(Although there was a moon this morning, a very fine one)
Or talk about doors closing when I mean heart seizure
(Although no doubt you shut the door when you left)
Nor refer in this season to a window opening
Nor of blind choking fog when I mean an adult crying
Crying, crying all night.
Oh no, if I want to say louse, pig or bastard
That people are bullies and like to watch others fall
On these broken pavements, and never lend a hand
Except to keep themselves up, I should say their names.

I will not watch the woodland lake dry up
"These four walls" I will say "and no one here."
(That's empty enough. The woman tried as hard
As anyone ever did. She bore no grudge
She didn't lie or nag. But so he left her
One lung and four kids; cotton dresses from the Summer.
He needed, he said, someone a little more cheerful.)
Nor hang-glide round the cloud crags of a sunset
"Light falling at such degree" I'll note "on cumulus.
Soon to be dark."
(When it is dark the people who have no homes
Become vagrants. When no business is doing
— Shops, libraries, offices, surgeries and bureaux —
They fall into a category of the dark:
Vagrant, not man or woman standing there.)
I will not listen to the wind in the yard what it says
(Tell me again: the voices I hear are lies.)

I'll give you these streets, these lives, these shops, straight.

                                                    Right?

The gobs and smelly flesh; the pleasant touch
Of people pleased to be warmed in bed; the fear
Of others taking what we yet might get; relief
Of the treadmill holding the foot again, secure.
And if someone is kind or beautiful
I will say so, and not talk of sunlight
Slanting down afternoon walls;
And the bustle and beams of lust in passers' eyes
Cherishing the day, quickening to the music
When other people play it, and the race in cars
Along the splashy roads and out and away:
The poise, the gearing, the rise in the blood and hopes,
Flick of a mobile wrist, swell of a breast
Shirt open on a pulse in a neck, warm breathing.

                               Ah no, we have gone too far
I said I would not talk of roads, of routes
Of night drives over the flanks of the land to the heart
Of a strange countryside in a hidden valley.
This town is on a map and it must stay here
One street much like another, and the hour
Of nine, say, on each day of the week the same.
Here's your piece of paper. Who lives here?

The town on the map has left out the dirt and the people
And the fact that things move, that daylight comes and dies,
That feelings waver in and out these hallways.
They have omitted to mark what the breath makes:
Islands and waving grasses; what the heart looks for
As sun makes shadows on an empty wall.
They do not know the corners which we round
Trudging home, our strength knocked out at the knees
Struck in the bone by circumstance; the ledges
That contain a whisper in the air about them
Matching some susurration in our blood
Which, while we feed it, says:

Piece of earth shoved here and there in the wind
Barged at by bullies, fostered here and there
Little thread weaving in and out of a day —
Citizen of this parish: the island, the hour;
Listen to the voices, watch the wall;
If you can hear my singing you are welcome.

Chrysanth

You see all those words thick on endless shelves
Stacked in their dust, thin poles in a forest stretching
Along straight lines marching to the horizon
Nothing but conifers covering the whole world
Black specks, leaves, words, squiggles on a white-board sky;

And you see that Chrysanthemum
Suddenly a pretty bob against a fence
New since I last was here?

It is the chrysanthemum I want.

Chrysanthemum is pretty
It clears the eye
Eases the brain
With wayward movement.

Wind comes, lashes, bedraggles;
Eye and joy dull.
Somewhere in these books, goddammit,
Unfurls, dancing —
Bringing back all still Autumn mornings
Bursting from those tight crowding pathless straight stems —
Luscious chrysanthemum.

Moon in the morning

Winter moon
You have sailed into the morning with me
Watched all the time I slept
Waited into the daylight till I could see you.
Prepared to lose your power
Miss your journey
In the face of day
And hung for one moment of clarity
Your open face into the open basin
Where night-being and day thoughts hold together in me —
Skin and silver water.
If now I look for you there is only pale blue and pretty
                                            peachy light
Steam and tiny traces of smoke
Clean in the air; and red and black roofs gleaming.
The day full of objects is scrambling our communication.
They have taken you down
The clear basin covered and dark now.

Waking

I am making a cave
I am making a cave out of
Out of the borders of sleep where daylight and birds
Push through the grey.
There is dancing and activity
And a fire that throws shifting shadows
On to the wall of the cave,
The cave that I'm clinging to
With every bit of my body.
I am trying to keep
I am trying to keep these shapes
These shapes I must fix, hold on to
But a great white smoke blows in.
"Cup of tea for you. Cup of tea. It's hot. Don't waste it."
I am hauled into empty day
Bereft of my dreams, of my story.

Waiting for a train in the early morning

Oh glorious sun, I
Have talked too much about you
Too often called your name
Too often sung your praises.

Here you are again
Sprung on this clean morning
Right into the sky
Your gong by none impeded
Nothing for miles and miles
But you: the light, the morning.

By midday back home
The whole sky will have shrivelled
The day will have filled with people
The buildings blocked the sky-line.
Here on urban land
As ugly as it comes
By chance this early morning
Sky has its occupant — sun —
Like any desert landscape.

Oh glorious sun
I have talked too much about you
Of your daily surprise
Of your endless returns.

"But they could <u>do</u> something about that."
(In praise of the Bourgeoisie)

The fragmentation of good gear is sad.
I am sorry to see the gold objects go
But some of them can be replaced, and of some
I have made replicas of steel which serve.

What I regret most
Are places not made pretty, plans
To fix things, and the pieces of wood, lying there
Till rotten. Talk of outings;
Syllabuses not books;
Pots still waiting for roses to ramble out of . . .
The dreamy primrose path so dreary-sided.

I think of Italians in cramped tenements
Making a hanging garden on rust-stained concrete.
If you look up the cliff from the alley well
Catching a glimpse of geranium, you sense a blue
Of hot sea shore, sniff a sparkle
Of windows opening across bays.
                              I think
Of people who clear their basements and lay carpets
Make fences and straight paths and box in pipes.
On a tin tray, dented and paint peeling,
The Japanese build a flourishing garden of ease
With little bits of glass.
They made belts out of sweet wrappers in the war.
They collected waste paper and it actually got to the depôt.

This house is full of half sets and broken tools.

House of the soul

The Summer is pouring through my windows
Sucking the house dry, burning off old Winters.
Paint flakes, timbers slacken
One more turn of the wheel in the house's ageing;
June at the year's Zenith
Powders the year up through a shaft of light
Pulls it along a tunnel of heat, upright.

They say old people get to look like their dogs.
Do they, I wonder, grow into their houses?
I and my house go through the seasons together

Rotting then drained, aged and balmed by the sun
Ex-hausted, by the sun's re-turning,
Of the sap that makes green wood unworkable.

And when the rains come, which they will,
What shadows, what life in the shadows,
Will the sun have stored in the corners of my house!

Tripping down (Scene: Another cold hillside)

I hold this goblet under the running tap
And it sparkles, being cut glass, and the droplets of water
                                        sparkle,
Beautiful as a chalice Morgan le Fay might bear.

But the water should be hot and isn't
I should have seen to the boiler
I should have done the washing
I should have eaten and not drunk.
Damned domestic skills
I would rather have Morgan's starveling ones.
How long can we live on cold water running over the rim
Of a beautiful goblet?
Ah, for a long time, I could, if holding it high
Running freezing over my hand with the boiler out
I was really looking into your beautiful blue cut-glass eyes
Instead of — old post-party trick — conjuring
Down the long tunnel of my own brown pebbles.

A patient old cripple

When I am out of sorts with the things
The world is made of, and box lids
Come off with a jerk sideways, scattering
The little things I can't pick up
Screws and buttons, bits of paper, pencils,

I think how I so loved the world once, as did someone else,
And remember hands that are beautiful — In pictures:
Soft and straight; fingers with tender pink nails;
And hips and legs an advantage, not crisis, in women.
Then I think
To birds my hands would not be hideous
A useful claw (they would see) not white
And strengthless and slabby and straight — so unprehensile.
The hand of my grandchild and mine are the same thing
As a word said differently is the same at root.
I curse the world that blunders into me, and hurts
But know
Its bad fit is the best that we can do.

Inverts

There was a woman
Who moved crablike
Humped in two directions, so bent
You'd think the front of her shoulder would graze the

pavement.

She pushed a cart
With four or five mangy scrabbling dogs hued,
Like her, colourless.

I never saw anyone help her at the curb
Nor carry the bag that pulled down her other arm.
Perhaps it balanced her or was fixed on.

On busy pavements there was always space round her.

Later I saw her without the dogs, more bent
As if some engine slowly wound her tighter.
Their removal had not helped her but perhaps Health
Had some consideration in plague-free streets.

I recall, though Spring is far away now, some buds
Are very curved and shrivelled, pale at first
And straighten into beautiful crisp flowers.

Oh idle beauties goldened in the sun
Do you not think your harsh and bitter laughs
May not wither and shrink those inner tendons
Fleshed now in comeliness and right proportions?

The little twisted woman trundles on
The young men sigh because they cannot move.

Not able to resist the Spring

There is too much stuff here:
Everything crowded, duplicated, and far too many words.
If I could just lay one silver blade across the sand
This would be your message —
One blue vault
One opposing ochre curve
One small man-made artefact drawing them together.

But I live in a crowded place
Myriads of wings and insects try for the sun
And the earth is traced and heaving with soft green spurs
That are uncontemplatable in terms of counting.
With all this buzz and batter and life drifting in clouds
                                        around me
Every breath full of mites and husks and voices
How can I only point one finger once?

Chorale

Oh what a syllabub
Hubbub
Bubbling and quetching of birds;
Of water gurgling
In gutters and chatter
And clatter of children
At break time over the wall;

And no doubt patter
Of insect legs drumming
Against twigs, in ricks
Of tickling straw
In this great appetite, this
Greedy maw
Called Spring,
Calling for more, for everything
To be up and doing
Like me like me like me
The blue tit insists;
And in the evening
Before the dark comes down
Again with a bit
Of Winter again
The blackbirds call
I am all yours
All yours, you-all.

Insolution

The air may be like wine
Or crisp lettuce
Or anything that is good for you.
April's showers, and wind,
Have brought down the cherry blossom
But left some snow clumps floating for a little longer;
Soft they would be to mouth if one were tall enough.
What has dropped looks messy in the gutter
But this is not a day to mind the litter.
I remember seeing far off across a green lawn many years ago
A clump of crocuses around an ancient tree,
What if, I thought, when we come nearer to it
It turns out to be orange peel in this swept pasture?

Browned blossom — or sodden sweet papers . . .
But "what is beauty?" is far too large a question
With a spring day like this one surging around me.

46

Letter to comfort a friend

No, I don't like the rain either;
Nor can I stand the litter.
Nor the gross purple letters slurred
Across fine outlines, and proud memorials.
Martyrs, lovers, scholars held
You should not mind the sneers or stones,
The armies ruining the land,
The destruction of temples:
Their love the stronger for it.
The walls of the world
Have always oppressed the spirit;
Plastic detritus the thumbscrew, so,
These yobs — the wheel.

There are more accidents in the home than on the roads

I remember hearing a story of a whole family
Destroyed in one go by a ring of a doorbell.
No, not electrocution, nor gun shot.
Like this:
The young mother was bathing the baby when the bell rang;
The toddler hastening to answer, fell down the stairs
Skull cracked on arrival; the mother ran to the screams;
The baby drowned.
It was a telegram, the door, to tell her
Her husband had been killed in an accident.

Well, old friend, this was your Northern humour
To bring, to pantomime level, such Greek disaster
Told in such a way I could disbelieve it.
But I thought of that dreadful tale when I heard this one:

A disappointed girl waited at home
Long past the days when he might possibly ring
The first man who'd said he would.

Heavy-hearted, empty, she dragged upstairs
And then, wild buzzing, the 'phone was actually ringing.
Frenzied, she dashed, and gasping picked it up
Ready with her joy. "Jane?" "Oh yes!"
"Would you like to suck my cock? It's a great big huge one."
Unlikely the stranger expected such blasts of tears.
Every time the 'phone rings she shakes with shame.

This day our daily . . . .

How many times have I counted my blessings in the baker's,
How many times not grumbled because-it-doesn't-help-anyone-
                                    does-it? with the butcher,
How many times counted the five little cats watching from
                                    the hedge
Of the lady who sweeps her path, who also watches?
Whatever the weather has been
"Bit better to-day, i'n't it?" the newsagent says
Heart breaking.

"Those were the . . . ."

Biro all over the sheets
Sleeves balled in sweat-stained armpits
Nylon socks threaded round tea towels.

She thinks of the white linen they used to have
Stiffened as wedding icing.
The perfect groomed men
Shooting glazed cuffs in fire-bright polished halls
Silk-socked tendons rising from unscratched leather;
The kitchen staff; the gatherings; baking day;
And women, no doubt, who came to do the sewing.
Perhaps there would be a dance or a marriage from it.

The machine comes to a halt
She puts down the magazine
And heaves the washing out.

Going to Sylvie's

The voice came loudly round the corner
"Now we're going to see Sylvie. Come along,"
Much louder than needed to instruct a child.
"What are you bringing me round here for, you see how I
                                    look after you,
I've got to follow your every step.
Just a minute here to please you then.
You see how gently I'm bringing you. You'll think of that."
No lumbering idiot boy or old deaf person led,
The sturdy middle-aged back, not ill-clothed
Bent again to say, so we heard across the morning common
"Now we're going to Sylvie's. You'll see
That'll be nice. You really must come along now"
To a black dog.

High life

The daft things people do
Appal me.
Look at that woman, an island in the traffic
Clutching a terrified child by the hand; that is
No education at all. He
Is spued over by diesel fumes and all she
Does is stand him in it.

The daft things people do
Amaze me.
Could I be the sort of person to carry a huge umbrella,
Striped, on that narrow pavement?
That big man's in a daze; he
Doesn't care a bit if anyone else can live.

Fancy having three dinners in one week cooked for me.
If only I could keep up my intentions
Formed on rum and beer to be unwise, be
Careless and a tornado, prize the

Feckless and raucous and larger than life —
Striped umbrellas and silly women — then
I would
Surprise me.

If you can't join them beat them

I have finished with saying I'm sorry and waiting
While badly-driven sports cars cross my path
Their thin-lipped drivers glaring and shouting "Fuck you!"
Nor do I lower my window now only to be harangued
By some yellow-eyed little runt who only knows
"You oughtn't to be on the road, you ought to be shot."

I content myself by thinking how they'll wear their pants out
Stuck to their seats encased in their only armour,
Fish that must flop on land, legs useless as penguins',
And that the pulse in their ticking cheeks probably means
Apoplexy at forty.
I used to boil in silence under the shock.
Now I open up the throttle and yell back.

Modern witches 1: crouching

As I stir this soup my powers come back to me,
As I grind this powder and mix my special paste
And polish with fury my ceremonial bowl.
Outraged man with Rover you will be sorry
For what you shouted at the traffic lights:
My curses bring on the freezing shadow of age
Harden those disagreeable runnels in your face;
May the usual destructions that are coming to you
Hit you with more than ordinary pain.
And you, rude woman, throwing your weight on children
Your bus the only place you boss, rheumatics
Twist your jabbing fingers before age does;

May the drip forever dangle on your nose.
Pompous doctor showing off to students
Fish-moving mouth will one day never quite shut
And apoplexy silence who once squashed many;
Patronizing dentist who tells lies
About drab patients' teeth, to get their fees
And leave town early Friday for golf with friends
(And midday Monday nurse tells moaning faces
"He is too busy, too busy, too greatly busy to see you")
May a nerve twitch in you no private practice
Can ever quell.
Pushers and shovers and sneerers and the square woman
Running the launderette for her chosen clients
(May you go round and round and up and down
And every time your squawking mouth shouts "Help!"
Let floods of soap rush in)
All the things I couldn't say to you
Have boiled up now into this bitter brew.

Back in my dominion I devise remedies.

The powerless ever pretended to be witches.

Modern witches 2: sentinels

I know what you're doing, you figures standing at gates,
Straight pillars for legs, encased in bandages
Thick orange stockings fixed in turquoise slippers.
Your hair is screwed to yellow-whitey curls
Showing pink patches, and your lips tight clamped.
There are more of you behind the curtained windows.
You stand there for longer than to say good evening
To those who pass. As I move
Beneath the messages that cross the street
You are measuring my back, and getting details:
My haircut, jacket, gear, and the mates I go with.
You pretend you are looking down the road for your man

To put the potatoes on, but you are communing
With the other hags and warlocks in this road
To lay a curse and muck up our motor-cycles.

Well, it's Friday night, and you wait till we roar round your
corner.
That ought to smash your spells.

Just a snack for lunch

This do here, by the window? The steak's not bad.
— Yes, Elspeth, please, and a carafe of red I think.
Brought my friend Jack to see you, so do your best. —
The service is good here — foreign. There used to be
A smashing German. My God, what a bottom!
Mixed grill for you? Well, I'll have steak as usual.
Always do on Friday. It's steak tonight
And what my wife calls steak — well, you couldn't see it.
"Treat for you tonight, dear" she's going to say
"You work so hard. Two lovely days at home."
And if I've had a fill-up at midday
I think of the plateful that I've had in here.
I close my eyes and sniff and smile at that.
She's very good, my wife. I don't know how
She manages the way she does. I'm grateful.
Thank God for the office grind and the lunch-hour rush.
Here comes the paté. Roll, Jack? Well, tuck in.

Visiting

We all go back with flowers
Well-fed, well rested.
Babies a year older
Wave bye-bye from all
The stations we stop at.

And yes, we will come again soon
To this upright life, these people:
Here we would recover.

Two minutes away from the station
The city throws its arms
Reflected in café doorways
Spilling on sleazy pavements
Music from lighted windows.
We sink to its solitudes.

Next time it will be the same
And the babies a year older.

Butcher's

White and silky neck with light brown curls
Soft like a calf's and a soft sparkly brown eye,
Will you in years become bristled and red —
Thick hanging neck of the slow-moving ox
The senior butcher you are learning from?
If you knew this, would you invite the axe
While you are still so young and palatable?

Sunripe

There are peaches, you know, and there are girls,
Girls who believed what their mothers told them
When they were talking to the clouds.

There are peaches, and there are people who eat peaches,
Sucking the juice, throwing the stone away.
Cannibals eat their enemies, not only for food
But to get their strength from the magic, from the blood.
Fruit eaters suck for the Good. Peach of a girl,
Glowing with all that a cannibal needs to revive him,
Peachy, take care.

Subscription

"Would you buy a flow-wer? Tenpence each for a flow-wer."
Little gypsy girl who spoke so nicely
Why would I not buy a flower and let you think
You had something worth selling?
Certainly they were of value, your paper flowers.
I could have stuck it somewhere, and I'm sure
It would have looked pretty if I thought it did.
Who am I not to buy worthless things?
I've squandered far more than tenpence on bad beer
And not embarrassed. We are so canny now
So tasteful and sensible only the real sharks get us.
Little grimy trader next time I see you
I'll buy a flower.
But soon you will be indoors with all the might
Of modern expertise whirling around you —
That we have given rivers and fields away for —
Making plastic tops for rotten pens
As give-aways with packets of washing powder.
We crunch them in the gutter every day
In the very street where you were peddling flowers.

Little dots

Little dots on paper stand as a letter
And letters at a glimpse exhale a sound
Which to our habit represents a thing.
I put the squiggles and a world appears.
If I write "numb" my toe hurts; "lick" — there's a dog.

Down from this stair window, little dots
Are moving and changing in the space below.
They step, they turn, and, focused, take an aspect.
These flecks turn into persons that like clothes,
Put tins on shelves, itch, fancy themselves,
Suck at their teeth and think it terribly important
Which saucers to choose and whether the carpet's dirty.

On my table a man's photograph
Is looking at me with intelligence.
I pass my hand across. He is not there.
I touch a shoulder and I say a name
Only as someone tells me we say so.
Freed from the block of flesh the picture knows me
Because the life I've given him is mine.
I look in his eye and I see only my eye.
It has no blood from which the steam arising
Muzzes the head.
                        A squiggle slanting one way
Suggests a bosom, we lean a head against it.
Another line, a parrot in a pet shop
Shouting at its owner.
So we make rise a landscape from our breath
And set a shaft of sun slanting across
A chair, with a man in it outside his door,
His soft cloth slippers waggling from his feet.

Little pieces that I meant to show
Who jog and weave, wandering like firework sparks
Splinters of flak reflecting in the dark,
You swim in clusters as we peer about,
There are thousands of you flung upon the night
Each of you also trying to work out pictures
Of what that dark is made of.
And out there somewhere spinning on their own
The pet-shop man, the drunken friend, the pisser,
Neighbours, kind over walls, clacking advice,
Old woman in tweed coat and white summer straw
Helped by a man with horse's teeth, all gum,
Laughing as they cross the road, where stands
Sixteen-year-old Apollo, still sticky-mouthed
Gazing into a shop at his reflection.

I stand at the stairwell looking out on the plain.
The whisper has sunk. I cannot hear the voices.
What ghosts have conjured me, I wonder, to lap my blood,

And what will anchor, beyond my sight perhaps,
The kite string that keeps us flying? To make our world
We need the untrapped minute, unwriteable,
The real chrysanthemum that stinks and rots,
The breath of lips that mists the good clean mirror,
A hand on our shoulder, someone saying our name.

56

Lure

Someone a long way off is using my blood.
Maybe sip-sipping it when they lap the rain,
Maybe not getting the extra nourishment,
Maybe not tasting, in glasses they drink, the iron.

How have they siphoned it off and made it run
That way, without knowing it, without adjusting the lode?
Maybe some strength would return from that provendered
                                                      flesh
If the face were to lift and show there, rising, my blood.

Veins that have used it pulse another way
The lymph that I need and they've taken is sluiced in the
                                                      yard.

Some strong light has got itself into my brain
But instead of glowing, pulls, as a black cloth does,
The soft white filament that holds together my head
And vacuums, unneedy, the threads from their lodge in my
                                                      mind.

On the far hill waves the luxuriant growth
Leaving this soil without its wanted food.

An instant on the viaduct

Moving at evening across the viaduct
On the regular train on ordinary business
The sun struck the side of the city before it sank
Leaving it flushed and softened when it had gone
And the bridge in the water fiery in the sunset.

The train stopped on the crossing, full, no doubt
Of cargo and equipment necessary
To provender the country, everything working
More or less well, wheels turning, people fed.

What if, I thought, I sprang from off this bridge
And floated into that tower that holds the light
Unmeshed by "should" and "next day" and "your health"?

The sky shifted and crept back. The train moved.
I cannot leave it; not for nothing
I am commander of this Capitol.

I dare not leave, and yet I dare not not,
For out there is what feeds the city's power
That building I almost touch across the air
And far beyond the reach of such as I.

The dark curtained us in. I do not act.
I wait. The tower will topple anyway.

Tug

When we started this game I had backers
Equal to the men who hold your rope.
I had a strong anchor man
And I had support in the galleries.

I find myself being jerked
Across the marked tiles, sliding.
My team is obviously slackening its hold.
Some have let go entirely, and of some
I cannot remember they were here.

There is little point in dislocating my shoulder, no hope
Of pulling all you six back to my side.
I am accelerated across, thread on a whirling bobbin
With only just time to think
Whether I should come across with a leap and a laugh or
Let go the rope.

On the Nature of Scientific Law

Newton watched a lot of balls
Flying through windows before he found
Beautiful in its general truth
The law that has no need of playthings —
Cricket bat lost, the apple long since rotten.

And so we move from rung to rung, or fall:
And get the view when our feet have left the ladder.
But I am attached to things, as a ladder to the ground.
I live off apples; the truth that climbs through me
Does not absorb the traces nor veil your face.

Figure in a landscape

A smell of burning like a noise erupts —
Doors slam and children chatter, wheel in, and fly
Off again like flocks of birds round fruit.
The machine hums and day turns out its thread.

Somewhere in this torrent is a place
Within the fall where a drop of water hearkens
Slowly on its own in the cave of water;
Takes the surroundings in and from its surface,
Tensed and unbroken, gives back the white spray rising.

The smashed cascade tumbles with fragments of day;
Somewhere you cannot touch behind the roaring
The coiling rope twists as one stream of water.

Somewhere within the house is a chamber of air
Where clearly, when you are gone, I see and hear you;
Where everything that I say perfects my sentence,
Where everything that you hear was my aim to say —
Each movement and outline remaining always the person.

But what we say through doors and on stairs, real
In a different way when bodies really stand there
Blurs the mirror with its actual breath.

A man's feet planted at the water's edge
Will join the mirrored body in the river:
Mirror of eyes produces the land within
The gazer's eyes, not rooted in outward objects.
The foil of my mind peels back when you are here
And your image plunges into the darkness there.

Upside down

We need a template. I have fixed on you.
When you withdraw the image will be there.
The blank becomes the object round which flows
Feeling, as ink prevented makes a shape.
And something of the truth will then seem clear
Readable edge against white, and in that outline
Uncharted waters defined by opposing shore.

The fire, died down, will leave deposit where
No heat comes out; this hardens into stone.
The earth, from this high up, becomes white vapour,
And these stupendous forests of cloud — the world.